D0319727

ICE LOLLIES
AND OTHER COOL TREATS

BY NANCY LAMBERT

PUBLISHING PLC

Published by Top That! Publishing plc
Tide Mill Way, Woodbridge, Suffolk, IP12 1AP, UK
www.topthatpublishing.com
Copyright © 2011 Top That! Publishing plc

CONTENTS

INTRODUCTION

The first record of an ice lolly being created was in 1905 by an eleven-year-old American boy named Frank Epperson. He left a glass of soda water powder and water outside his house with a wooden mixing stick in it. That night, the temperature dropped to below freezing and when Frank woke up the next morning, he found that the soda water had frozen inside the glass. He was able to remove the ice from the glass with the mixing stick and eat it – the first ever ice lolly!

Since then, cool cooking has grown in popularity and often there's nothing better than cooling down on a hot day with an ice cold lolly, a refreshing cool drink or a delicious bowl of ice cream.

You can make popsicles, ice creams and sorbets from almost any ingredient you choose! This book will provide you with a selection of cool recipes, each one bursting with fun and flavour. And remember, once you have perfected the recipes, don't be afraid to experiment with ingredients, moulds and toppings to create your own great ice cool treats!

Cool Cooking Tips!
- Make sure you use the freshest ingredients available.
- Ingredients expand when freezing, so when making popsicles, leave 1 cm at the top of each mould.
- Pour the ingredients into the moulds or trays carefully – use jugs or spouted containers.
- Ingredients take a while to freeze. Plan ahead so you have plenty of time.
- Make room for your moulds, trays and tubs in the freezer.
- Remember, you can freeze any of the cool drinks in this book! Just pour into ice lolly moulds and place into a freezer for 4 hours, or until solid.

EQUIPMENT

- To complete the recipes in this book, you will need to use a selection of everyday cooking equipment and utensils, such as mixing bowls, saucepans, a sieve, knives, spoons and forks and a chopping board.

- Of course, you'll need to weigh and measure the ingredients, so you'll need a measuring jug and some kitchen scales too.

- Some of the recipes tell you to use a whisk. Ask an adult to help you use an electric whisk, or you can use a balloon whisk yourself – you'll just have to work extra hard!

- To make some of the recipes in this book, you'll need to use the correct-sized tins or other special equipment. These items (and others that you may not have to hand) are listed at the start of each recipe.

SAFETY & HYGIENE

- Before starting any cooking always wash your hands.

- Cover any cuts with a plaster.

- Wear an apron to protect your clothes.

- Always make sure that all the equipment you use is clean.

- If you need to use a sharp knife to cut up something hard, ask an adult to help you. Always use a chopping board.

- Remember that trays in the oven and pans on the cooker can get very hot. Always ask an adult to turn on the oven and to get things in and out of the oven for you.

- Always ask an adult for help if you are using anything electrical – like an electric whisk.

- Be careful when heating anything in a pan on top of the cooker. Keep the handle turned to one side to avoid accidentally knocking the pan.

- Keep your pets out of the kitchen while cooking.

ADULT SUPERVISION IS REQUIRED FOR ALL RECIPES

GETTING STARTED

MEASURING

Use scales to weigh exactly how much of each ingredient you need or use a measuring jug to measure liquids.

MIXING

Use a spoon, balloon whisk or electric hand whisk to mix the ingredients together.

DIFFERENT IDEAS

Decorate your ice cream and sundaes with chocolate drops, sweets or sugar strands. Ice lollies can be made from almost any ingredients you choose! Why not substitute some of the ingredients to make your own special recipes!

DIFFERENT SHAPES

Ice lolly moulds come in lots of different shapes and sizes, and can be bought from most large supermarkets.

CREATING RECIPES

Once you've made a recipe in this book a few times, think about whether you could make your own version. This way you can start to make up your own recipes. Try to think up names for the things you create!

PLEASE NOTE

The measurements given in this book are approximate. Use the same measurement conversions throughout your recipe (grams or ounces) to maintain the correct ratios. All of the recipes in this book have been created for adults to make with junior chefs and must not be attempted by an unsupervised child.

The 'Makes …' label is a guide only and will differ depending on the size of the mould or tray.

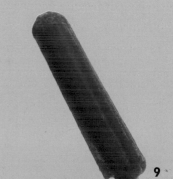

FRUITY STICKS

Extra equipment:
- blender
- ice lolly moulds

Ingredients:
- 200 g (7 oz) of your favourite fruit e.g blackcurrants, oranges etc
- 225 ml (8 fl.oz) natural yogurt or good quality fruit yogurt
- 225 ml (8 fl.oz) water
- 3 tablespoons icing sugar

1 Wash and prepare the fruit to start with. Chop your chosen fruit.

2 Place into the blender, along with the yogurt, water and sugar and blend until smooth. (If you have not got a blender, place the ingredients into a bowl and ask an adult to blend the mixture with a hand-held electric whisk.)

3 Tip the mixture into a jug, and then pour into lolly moulds. Put the moulds into a freezer and let them set for at least 4 hours, until solid.

4 Remove the lollies from the freezer and let them stand at room temperature for 5 minutes. Then, remove from the moulds and enjoy!

TOP TIP!
Try experimenting with different fruit or a combination of fruit to make different coloured lollies and create a whole array of colourful pops!

BERRY POPS

Extra equipment:

- blender
- ice lolly moulds

Ingredients:

- 225 g (8 oz) fresh mixed berries
- 50 g (2 oz) icing sugar
- 2 tablespoons clear honey
- 2 tablespoons lemon juice
- 900 ml (1 ½ pt) natural yogurt

1 Put all of the ingredients in a blender, reserving a few of the smaller berries for later. Ask an adult to process the mixture until smooth. (If you have not got a blender, place the ingredients into a bowl and ask an adult to blend the mixture with a hand-held electric whisk.)

2 Now add the reserved smaller berries to the mixture and pour into the lolly moulds. Place the moulds into a freezer.

3 When the mixture has partially frozen, rotate the moulds – this way the larger pieces of fruit won't clump together. Leave them to set for at least 4 hours, until solid.

4 Remove the lollies from the freezer and let them stand at room temperature for 5 minutes. Then, remove from the moulds and enjoy!

TOP TIP!
Any leftover mixture can be made into a smoothie! Just blitz it in a blender with some more yogurt and milk if it's too thick!

CITRUS BURSTS

Extra equipment:
• ice lolly moulds

Ingredients:
• 100 ml (3 fl.oz) strong lemon or pineapple cordial or fruit juice
• 100 ml (3 fl.oz) strong orange cordial or fruit juice
• food colouring (optional)

1 Pour the first cordial into the ice lolly moulds, along with a splash of water, until each mould is about half full.

2 Place the moulds into the freezer and leave them to set for at least 4 hours, until solid.

3 Repeat the process, but this time with the different-flavoured cordial. Pour on top of the frozen layer and place into the freezer, until solid.

4 Remove the lollies from the freezer and let them stand at room temperature for 5 minutes. Then, remove from the moulds and enjoy!

TOP TIP!
Change the juice to make different coloured pops or add a couple of drops of food colouring to make them really bright!

STRAWBERRY MILKSHAKE STICKS

Extra equipment:
• lolly moulds

Ingredients:
• 350 ml (12 fl.oz) milk
• 2 teaspoons strawberry milkshake powder
• handful of redcurrants

1 Pour the milk into a measuring jug until it reaches 350 ml (12 fl.oz). Add the strawberry powder into the milk, and stir well.

2 Pour into the lolly moulds, along with a few redcurrants. Put the moulds into a freezer and let them set for at least 4 hours, until solid.

3 Remove the lollies from the freezer and let them stand at room temperature for 5 minutes. Then, remove from the moulds and enjoy!

TOP TIP!
Use full-fat milk for a creamy taste!

RASPBERRY STICKS

Extra equipment:
- sieve
- ice lolly moulds

Ingredients:
- 300 g (10 1/2 oz) raspberries
- 200 g (7 oz) clear honey
- juice of 1 lemon

1 Ask an adult to heat the raspberries in a pan, along with the honey and lemon juice.

2 Allow the mixture to come to a boil and then remove from the heat.

3 Stir and mash the raspberries with a wooden spoon and then push the mixture through a sieve to get rid of the pips.

4 Leave the mixture to cool and then pour into the lolly moulds. Put the moulds into a freezer and let them set for at least 4 hours, until solid.

5 Remove the lollies from the freezer and let them stand at room temperature for 5 minutes. Then, remove from the moulds and enjoy!

TOP TIP! Double the ingredients and make lots of lollies. Great for when your friends come round!

PARTY POPS

Extra equipment:
• ice lolly moulds

Ingredients:
• 1 litre (1 3/4 pt) lemonade
• food colouring

1 Fill each of the moulds with lemonade, followed by a couple of drops of food colouring. Use as many different colours as you like for a varied effect.

2 Give the moulds a stir, then put them into a freezer and let them set for at least 4 hours, until solid.

3 Remove the lollies from the freezer and let them stand at room temperature for 5 minutes. Then, remove from the moulds and enjoy!

TOP TIP!
These pops will keep you nice and hydrated in the hot summer months! Arrange them in a bucket of ice to serve!

CHOC POPS

Extra equipment:
- jug
- ice lolly moulds

Ingredients:
- 60 g (2 oz) milk chocolate
- 3 tablespoons natural yogurt
- 6 drops vanilla extract
- 2 tablespoons milk

1 Ask an adult to put a heatproof bowl over a saucepan of just-simmering water, making sure the bowl doesn't touch the water. Break the milk chocolate into small pieces and put them into the bowl. Stir the mixture until the chocolate has melted.

2 Pour the melted chocolate into a jug and add the remaining ingredients. Stir, then leave to cool. Once cool, pour the mixture into the ice lolly moulds.

3 Put the moulds into a freezer and allow to set for at least 4 hours, until solid.

4 Remove the lollies from the freezer and let them stand at room temperature for 5 minutes. Then, remove from the moulds and enjoy!

TOP TIP! Add 2 chopped bananas to the mixture for Banana and Chocolate Pops!

16

COCONUT MILK ICE

Extra equipment:
• ice lolly moulds

Ingredients:
• 350 ml (12 fl.oz) milk
• 100 g (4 oz) caster sugar
• 1 teaspoon vanilla extract
• 750 ml (1 ½ pt) coconut milk

1 Ask an adult to place the milk and sugar in a pan and heat until the sugar dissolves.

2 Next, stir in the vanilla extract and leave to cool.

3 Pour the mixture into a bowl and add the coconut milk.

4 Then, pour the mixture into the lolly moulds. Place the moulds into a freezer and leave them to set for at least 4 hours, until solid.

5 Remove the lollies from the freezer and let them stand at room temperature for 5 minutes. Then, remove from the moulds and enjoy!

TOP TIP! Why not add some mashed banana to the mixture for coconut and banana ice?

CHEEKY CHERRY POPS

Extra equipment:
- blender
- ice lolly moulds

Ingredients:
- 1 litre (1 ¾ pt) still water
- 6 tablespoons cherry extract
- 260 g (9 oz) cherries, stoned

1 Ask an adult to place all of the ingredients into a blender and process until smooth.

2 Next, pour the cherry mixture into the ice lolly moulds. Place the moulds into a freezer and leave them to set for at least 4 hours, until solid.

3 Remove the lollies from the freezer and let them stand at room temperature for 5 minutes. Then, remove from the moulds and enjoy!

TOP TIP!
Add a few blueberries to the blended mixture for an even fruitier treat!

JUICY TANGERINE POPS

Extra equipment:
- juicer
- ice lolly moulds

Ingredients:
- 450 g (1 lb) tangerines

1 First, you will need to extract the juice from the tangerines. Either ask an adult to place the tangerines in a juicer, or cut the tangerines in half and squeeze the juice out of them, making sure that there are no pips.

2 Pour the juice into the lolly moulds. Place the moulds into a freezer and leave them to set for at least 4 hours, until solid.

3 Remove the lollies from the freezer and let them stand at room temperature for 5 minutes. Then, remove from the moulds and enjoy!

TOP TIP!
Add some fresh chopped pineapple to the juice to give the pops some bulk and texture! Just place in a blender and add to the tangerine juice.

ORANGE, STRAWBERRY & MANGO POPS

Extra equipment:
- blender
- ice lolly moulds

Ingredients:
- 1 mango
- 350 ml (12 fl.oz) orange juice
- handful of strawberries, washed and hulled

1 Ask an adult to prepare the mango. Slice the cheeks of the mango from either side of the stone, and score the flesh in a criss-cross pattern to the skin. Push the skin up, pushing the flesh out. The flesh can then be sliced easily away from the skin. Tip the flesh into a blender, along with any juices.

2 Next, put the rest of the ingredients into the blender, and ask an adult to process the mixture until smooth. (If you have not got a blender, place the ingredients into a bowl and ask an adult to blend the mixture with a hand-held electric whisk.)

3 Pour the mixture into the lolly moulds. Place the moulds into a freezer and leave them to set for at least 4 hours, until solid.

4 Remove the lollies from the freezer and let them stand at room temperature for 5 minutes. Then, remove from the moulds and enjoy!

TOP TIP! Packed full of goodness, this ice lolly makes a great, healthy snack! Make sure you wash the fruit before using.

COLA POPS

Extra equipment:
• ice lolly moulds

Ingredients:
• 350 ml (12 fl.oz) cola

1 Fill each of the moulds with cola.

2 Put the moulds into a freezer and let them set for at least 4 hours, until solid.

3 Remove the lollies from the freezer and let them stand at room temperature for 5 minutes. Then, remove from the moulds and enjoy!

TOP TIP! Add a splash of cherry juice or cherry flavoured cordial to make cherry cola pops!

BERRY ICE CUBES

MAKES 12-15

Extra equipment:
- ice cube tray

Ingredients:
- 350 ml (12 fl.oz) water
- handful of small berries,
  i.e blueberries, cranberries etc
  or larger berries,
  i.e strawberries cut in half

1 Ask an adult to boil a kettle and then let it cool. Pour the cooled water into the ice cube tray. (Ice made from boiled water turns out clear, rather than cloudy.)

2 Next, pick which berries you would like to use. (Small berries can be whole, or chop fruit such as strawberries and raspberries into pieces.)

3 Drop a piece of fruit carefully into the water of each section in the ice cube tray.

4 Place the ice cube tray into a freezer and let the cubes set for at least 4 hours, until solid.

5 Remove the ice cubes from the tray and enjoy, either on their own or in a cool drink!

TOP TIP! Don't be afraid to experiment! Why not add citrus zest or sweets to your ice cubes?

COLOURFUL ICE CUBES

Extra equipment:
• ice cube tray

Ingredients:
• 350 ml (12 fl.oz) water
• splash of fruit cordial or a few drops of food colouring

1 Ask an adult to boil a kettle and then let it cool. Pour the cooled water into the ice cube tray. (Ice made from boiled water turns out clear, rather than cloudy.)

2 Next, add either a splash of fruit cordial to each cube or a drop of food colouring to make the cubes colourful.

3 Place the ice cube tray into a freezer and let the cubes set for at least 4 hours, until solid.

4 Remove the ice cubes from the tray and enjoy, either on their own or in a cool drink!

TOP TIP!
Alternate with different colours to create a rainbow of ice cubes!

23

LEMONADE

MAKES APPROX 1 LITRE

Extra equipment:
- heatproof jug
- sieve

Ingredients:
- 4 unwaxed lemons, washed
- 100 g (4 oz) caster sugar
- 570 ml (1 pt) boiling water
- 400 ml (13 1/2 fl.oz) chilled still water
- ice, crushed

1 Ask an adult to grate the zest from the lemons, leaving as much white pith behind as possible.

2 Half the lemons, then squeeze the juice into a large heatproof jug. Also, place the zest and sugar into the jug.

3 Pour in 570 ml (1 pt) of boiling water and stir until the sugar has dissolved. Cover, and leave to cool completely.

4 Now, strain the mixture into a serving jug, and discard the zest. Dilute with the chilled water and sweeten with extra sugar to taste.

5 Serve decorated with lemon slices and crushed ice.

TOP TIP! Add a pinch of lime zest as well for an added citrus kick!

FRUITY PUNCH

Ingredients:

- 1 litre (34 fl.oz) cranberry juice
- 500 ml (17 fl.oz) orange juice
- 250 ml (8 ½ fl.oz) lemon juice
- 100 ml (3 fl.oz) ginger ale
- ice cubes
- a selection of fresh fruit:
  strawberries
  seedless grapes
  pieces of kiwi
  pieces of orange
  pieces of mango
  pieces of banana
  pieces of pineapple
- sprig of mint, to decorate

1 Wash and prepare the fruit and ask an adult to chop them into chunks.

2 Pour the cranberry, orange, and lemon juice into a large jug or bowl to make a punch.

3 Stir the chopped fruit into the punch and pour in the ginger ale.

4 Tip in the ice cubes and serve the punch in glasses, garnished with sliced fruit and a sprig of mint!

TOP TIP!
Double the ingredients and keep another jugful in the fridge – this will be drunk so quick you'll need a reserve!

25

SAN FRANCISCO

Extra equipment:
• sieve

Ingredients:
• 50 ml (1 ½ fl.oz) fresh orange juice
• 50 ml (1 ½ fl.oz) fresh lemon juice
• 50 ml (1 ½ fl.oz) fresh pineapple juice
• 50 ml (1 ½ fl.oz) fresh grapefruit juice
• 1 tablespoon non-alcoholic grenadine
• soda water
• lemon, lime and orange slices (optional)

1 Pour all of the ingredients, apart from the soda and optional lemon, lime and orange slices, into a jug and stir well.

2 Add ice, then strain through a sieve into a glass.

3 Top with soda water, then garnish with lemon, lime and orange slices.

4 Serve and drink immediately!

TOP TIP! Experiment with different juices and see which combination you like best!

26

PINK LEMONADE

Extra equipment:
- blender
- sieve

Ingredients:
- 3 unwaxed lemons
- 100 g (4 oz) sugar, more or less, depending on taste
- 1 litre (2 pt) water, still or sparkling
- 120 ml (4 fl.oz) cranberry juice
- ice cubes
- 1 unwaxed lemon, sliced

1 First, ask an adult to cut the lemons, including the skin, but not the ends, into rough chunks.

2 Pile the lemons into a blender with 25 g (1 oz) of sugar and enough still water to almost cover them. Ask an adult to process to a mush.

3 Then, strain through a sieve. Return the mush to the blender and add another 25 g (1 oz) of sugar and more water. Keep repeating the process, adding the sieved juice to the first amount of liquid.

4 Taste the mixture and stir in more sugar or top up with sparkling water, depending on how sweet or tangy you like your drinks.

5 Pour the lemonade into a jug, and add the cranberry juice to make it pink.

6 Add ice cubes and serve with a slice of lemon.

TOP TIP! Crush the ice cubes by putting them in a plastic bag, then bash gently with a rolling pin.

CRANBERRY KISS

Extra equipment:
• blender

Ingredients:
• 3 handfuls strawberries
• 1 small banana
• 150 ml (5 fl.oz) cranberry juice
• 225 ml (7 ½ fl.oz) natural yogurt
• handful of cranberries
• 8 ice cubes, crushed

1 Wash and prepare the fruit to start with. Ask an adult to chop the strawberries and slice the banana into small pieces.

2 Place all of the ingredients in a blender and ask an adult to whizz until smooth. (If you have not got a blender, place the ingredients into a bowl and ask an adult to blend the mixture with a hand-held whisk.)

3 Pour into two glasses.

4 Top with a handful of cranberries, then drink immediately.

TOP TIP! Experiment with your choice of fruit topping. Blackcurrants are especially good!

STRAWBERRY SUNRISE

Extra equipment:
• blender

Ingredients:
• 3 handfuls strawberries
• 1 mango
• 350 ml (12 fl.oz) cranberry juice
• 4 ice cubes, crushed
• 1 scoop strawberry ice cream (see home-made recipe on page 47 or use shop-bought)
• handful of fresh raspberries or strawberries (optional)

1 Wash the fruit to start with. Ask an adult to chop the strawberries and prepare the mango.

2 Slice the cheeks of the mango from either side of the stone, and score the flesh in a criss-cross pattern to the skin. Push the skin up, pushing the flesh out. These can then be easily sliced away from the skin. Tip the flesh into a blender with any juices.

3 Place the remaining ingredients in a blender and ask an adult to whizz until smooth. (If you have not got a blender, place the ingredients into a bowl and ask an adult to blend the mixture with a hand-held whisk.)

4 Pour into two glasses.

5 Top with a scoop of strawberry ice cream and a couple of raspberries or strawberries.

6 Drink immediately.

TOP TIP! Pick the juiciest, ripest mango you can find and save some for later!

29

BANANA BURST

Extra equipment:
• blender

Ingredients:
• 2 bananas
• 350 ml (12 fl.oz) coconut milk
• a large dash of maple syrup
• 4 ice cubes, crushed

1 Peel the banana and ask an adult to slice it into small chunks.

2 Next, place all of the ingredients in a blender and whizz until smooth. (If you have not got a blender, place the ingredients into a bowl and ask an adult to blend the mixture with a hand-held whisk.)

3 Pour into two glasses.

4 Drink immediately.

TOP TIP!
Top the glass with dessicated coconut for an exotic twist!

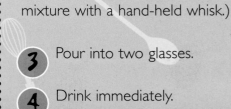

30

VAMPIRE'S BREATH

Extra equipment:
• blender

Ingredients:
• 1 handful blackcurrants
  (or forest fruits)
• 350 ml (12 fl.oz) lemonade
• dash of blackcurrant cordial
• 3 scoops vanilla ice cream
  (see home-made recipe on
  p.46 or use shop-bought)
• mint leaves, to decorate
  (optional)

1 First, wash the berries.

2 Then, place all of the ingredients in a blender, reserving a handful of blackcurrants for decoration, and ask an adult to whizz until smooth. (If you have not got a blender, place the ingredients into a bowl and ask an adult to blend the mixture with a hand-held whisk.)

3 Pour into two glasses, and top with blackcurrants.

4 Garnish with mint leaves (optional) for a fragrant finish. Serve immediately.

TOP TIP!
Decorate the glasses with spooky figures for a gruesome Halloween smoothie!

MUD PIE

Extra equipment:
• blender

Ingredients:
• 4 scoops chocolate ice cream (see home-made recipe on p.48 or use shop-bought)
• 350 ml (12 fl.oz) milk
• dash chocolate syrup
• 50 g (2 oz) milk chocolate, grated

1 Place the milk, 2 scoops of ice cream and the dash of chocolate syrup into a blender and ask an adult to whizz until smooth. (If you have not got a blender, place the ingredients into a bowl and ask an adult to blend the mixture with a hand-held whisk.)

2 Pour into two glasses.

3 Top with the remaining 2 scoops of ice cream, and sprinkle grated chocolate on top.

4 Serve immediately.

TOP TIP!
Pour chocolate syrup on top to create a muddy puddle topping.

32

SHIPWRECK

Extra equipment:
• blender

Ingredients:
• 1 pineapple
• 375 ml (12 fl.oz) milk
• 375 ml (12 fl.oz) pineapple yogurt
• 3 scoops vanilla ice cream (see home-made recipe on p.46 or use shop-bought)

1 Ask an adult to prepare the pineapple. First, remove the leafy top and the base. Then, slice the skin away, from top to bottom. Cut the pineapple in half, then into thick wedges. Remove the central core and then chop the wedges into small pieces.

2 Place all of the ingredients into a blender, reserving slices of pineapple for decoration, and ask an adult to whizz until smooth. (If you have not got a blender, place the ingredients into a bowl and ask an adult to blend the mixture with a hand-held whisk.)

3 Pour into two glasses, and decorate with pineapple slices.

4 Serve immediately.

TOP TIP! Serve with pirate's treasure – coconut shells filled with small sweets.

FRUITY FUN ICE CREAM SUNDAE

Extra equipment:
- blender
- sieve

Ingredients:
- 2 very ripe peaches
- 300 g (10 oz) ripe raspberries
- juice of half a lemon
- 25-50 g (1-2 oz) icing sugar
- 4 scoops vanilla ice cream (see home-made recipe on p.46 or use shop-bought)
- 150 ml (5 fl.oz) whipped cream
- 1 tablespoon toasted almonds (optional)
- 4 mint leaves, to decorate

1 Ask an adult to cut around the peach and down to the stone. Gently twist to remove the stone and halve the peaches.

2 Next, ask an adult to drop the peaches into boiling water for 8–10 seconds, lift out and place in cold water. Slip the skins off, keeping the peach halves intact.

3 Place the raspberries in a blender and ask an adult to liquefy them with a little lemon juice and icing sugar. Strain carefully through a sieve to remove the seeds.

4 To serve, place a small ball of vanilla ice cream in a glass and gently press a peach half on top. Carefully spoon the fresh raspberry sauce over the peach.

5 Repeat for the other portions.

6 Decorate with whipped cream, toasted almonds and mint leaves.

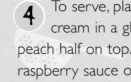

WARNING! Contains nuts.

STRAWBERRY ICE CREAM SUNDAE

Extra equipment:
- .blender
- sieve
- piping bag

Ingredients:
- 100 g (4 oz) strawberries
- 25 g (1 oz) icing sugar
- 1 teaspoon water
- 4 scoops strawberry ice cream
  (see home-made recipe on
  p.47 or use shop-bought)
- 75 ml (3 fl.oz) whipped cream
- handful of chopped walnuts,
  to decorate (optional)
- wafer stick, to decorate
  (optional)

1 Ask an adult to purée most of the strawberries in a blender with the icing sugar and 1 teaspoon of water.

2 Then, carefully push the resulting purée through a sieve to remove the seeds.

3 Pour a small amount of purée into the bottom of a sundae glass, then follow by piling a scoop of strawberry ice cream and a tablespoon of whipped cream. Repeat the process.

4 Spoon the remaining whipped cream on top of the sundae. Finish with a whole strawberry, a sprinkling of chopped walnuts and a wafer stick.

WARNING!
Contains
nuts.

SERVES 4

Extra equipment:

• silicone paper

• sieve

Ingredients:

• 115 g (4 oz) butter

• 70 g (2 ½ oz) caster sugar

• 165 g (5 ½ oz) plain flour

• 15 g (½ oz) rice flour

• 4 scoops vanilla ice cream
  (see home-made recipe on
  p.46 or use shop-bought)

• 480 g (1 lb) strawberries

1 Preheat the oven to 200°C / 400°F / gas mark 6.

2 Cream the butter and sugar together until light.

3 Sieve in the plain flour and rice flour and add to the butter mix. Mix together to make a smooth paste, then cover and chill.

4 Divide the mixture into eight even-sized balls and roll on sheets of silicone paper. Bake in a preheated oven until crisp and golden.

5 As soon as they are baked, sprinkle with a little more caster sugar whilst still hot.

6 When the shortcake is cold, use them to sandwich small balls of vanilla ice cream.

7 Alternate with halves of small strawberries. Decorate the tops with more ice cream and a halved strawberry to finish.

TOP TIP!
Experiment with different fruits and alternative ice cream flavours!

LEMON MOUSSE

Extra equipment:

- electric whisk
- 4 dessert glasses

Ingredients:

- 300 ml (10 fl.oz) double cream
- 1 lemon, juice and zest
- 50 g (2 oz) caster sugar
- 2 fresh egg whites (pasteurised if possible)
- 15 g (½ oz) chopped pistachios or almonds (optional)

1 Put the cream, lemon zest and sugar into a large bowl and ask an adult to whisk them together until the mixture starts to thicken.

2 Add the lemon juice and whisk again until the mixture thickens further. Be careful – the mixture must not be too thick for the next step.

3 Next, place the egg whites in a separate bowl and ask an adult to whisk until they form soft peaks. Fold them into the lemon mixture.

4 Spoon the mixture into the four glasses and chill in the refrigerator.

5 Decorate with extra lemon zest and the chopped pistachios.

WARNING! Contains nuts.

37

WHITE CHOCOLATE PISTACHIO MOUSSE

SERVES 4

Extra equipment:
- electric whisk
- 4 dessert glasses

Ingredients:
- 3 tablespoons water
- a few drops of vanilla essence
- 180 g (6 oz) white chocolate, grated
- 2 separated, fresh eggs (pasteurised if possible)
- 300 ml (10 fl.oz) whipping cream
- 45 g (1 ½ oz) pistachio nuts, chopped
- whole pistachio nuts, to decorate
- 45 g (1 ½ oz) white chocolate, grated, to decorate

1 Place the water, vanilla essence and white chocolate in a bowl over a second bowl filled with hot water until the chocolate has melted. Stir until smooth, then whisk in the egg yolks.

2 In a clean bowl, whisk the egg whites until they make soft peaks.

3 Lightly beat the cream and fold two thirds into the chocolate mixture, followed by the egg whites.

4 Place a spoonful in the bottom of four glasses. Sprinkle with chopped pistachios, then add another layer of mousse. Alternate mousse and pistachio layers until the glasses are full.

5 Finish whipping the remaining cream and place a spoonful on the top of each glass.

6 Decorate with whole pistachios and grated white chocolate to finish.

TOP TIP!
Keep the mousses in the fridge until they are ready to be eaten!

38

CHOCOLATE MOUSSE

Extra equipment:
- 4 dessert glasses

Ingredients:
- 100 g (4 oz) dark chocolate
- 2 separated, fresh eggs (pasteurised if possible)
- 300 ml (10 fl.oz) double cream
- 50 g (2 oz) caster sugar
- milk chocolate shavings, to decorate
- 15 g ($\frac{1}{2}$ oz) icing sugar, to decorate
- 4 mint leaves, to decorate

1 Melt the chocolate in a heatproof bowl over a pan of hot water. Make sure the water doesn't touch the bottom of the bowl.

2 Stir until smooth. Take the bowl off the heat and stir in the egg yolks.

3 Lightly beat the cream and fold two thirds into the melted chocolate.

4 Whip together the egg whites and sugar until they form soft peaks, and gently fold into the chocolate mixture.

5 Spoon the mixture into four glasses.

6 Next, finish whipping the remaining cream and add one neat spoonful to each mousse.

7 Finish the dish with a mint leaf, chocolate shavings and a dust of icing sugar.

TOP TIP!
Why not try milk or white chocolate – they work just as well!

39

PEACH SORBET

SERVES 6-8

Extra equipment:
• blender
• ice cream maker (optional)

Ingredients:
• 1 kg (2 lb 2 oz) peeled and
  diced fresh peaches, and their
  juice, reserving some for
  decoration
• 180 ml (6 fl.oz) lemon juice
• 250 g (9 oz) sugar
• 5 tablespoons orange juice
• sprig of mint, to decorate

1 Ask an adult to place the peaches into a blender and whizz until smooth.

2 Heat the remaining ingredients in a saucepan over a low heat until the sugar has dissolved. Remove from the heat and stir in the peach purée.

3 Pour the mixture into an ice cream maker and churn until frozen. Alternatively, if you don't have an ice cream maker you can freeze your sorbet in a plastic tub in the freezer. You will need to stir the mixture every hour to break up any ice.

4 To serve, scoop into small dishes and garnish with fresh peach slices and a sprig of mint.

TOP TIP!
Choose peaches that are soft to the touch with a heady sweet perfume – these are truly ripe.

LEMON SORBET

Extra equipment:
• ice cream maker (optional)

Ingredients:
• 450 g (1 lb) caster sugar
• 750 ml (1 ¼ pt) water
• 250 ml (9 fl.oz) lemon juice (6-8 lemons)
• mint leaves, to decorate

1 Ask an adult to pour the sugar into a pan with 750 ml (1 ¼ pt) of water. Heat gently until the sugar dissolves, then simmer for a couple of minutes.

2 Stir in the lemon juice and then grate one of the lemon skins. Add the zest to the mixture, then leave to cool.

3 Pour the mixture into an ice cream maker and churn until frozen. Alternatively, if you don't have an ice cream maker you can freeze your sorbet in a plastic tub in the freezer. You will need to stir the mixture every hour to break up any ice.

4 Scoop the lemon sorbet into a bowl. Add a slice of fresh lemon and mint leaves for decoration.

TOP TIP!
Why not use the leftover lemon pulp for the lemonade recipe on p.24?

LAYERED LOLLIES

TOP TIP!
Use 2 drops of food colouring in each stage to make the colours really pop!

MAKES 8–10

Extra equipment:
- blender
- ice lolly moulds
- sieve
- jug

Ingredients:
- 200 g (7 oz) blackcurrants
- 100 g (4 oz) caster sugar
- grated zest and juice of 1 unwaxed lemon
- 375 ml (12 fl.oz) water
- 1 green apple, cut into chunks
- 5 tablespoons lemon juice
- 1 tablespoon icing sugar
- 550 ml (1 pt) apple juice
- 255 g (9 oz) strawberries, washed and hulled
- 1 1/2 tablespoons clear honey

1 Place the blackcurrants, sugar, lemon zest and lemon juice in a saucepan with 75 ml (3 fl.oz) water. Heat gently, stirring until the sugar dissolves, then bring to the boil. Simmer gently for 5 minutes then allow to cool.

2 Ask an adult to add the mixture to a blender and process until smooth. Stir in 300 ml (9 fl.oz) of water. Tip the mixture into a jug, then pour into the lolly moulds, filling them up to about a third. Freeze for at least 4 hours, until solid.

3 Next, place the chopped apple in a saucepan along with 5 tablespoons of lemon juice, a tablespoon of icing sugar and the apple juice. Heat for 3–5 minutes, then transfer to a bowl to cool. Ask an adult to blend the mixture until smooth.

4 Tip the mixture into a jug, then pour into the lolly moulds on top of the blackcurrant layer, again filling them up to about a third. Freeze for at least 4 hours, until solid.

5 For the last layer, ask an adult to purée the strawberries in a blender, then push the purée through a sieve to remove the pips. Stir the honey into the purée. Then, pour the purée into each of the lolly moulds on top of the other frozen layers. Again, leave to set for at least 4 hours, until solid.

6 Remove the lollies from the freezer and let them stand at room temperature for 5 minutes. Then, remove from the moulds and enjoy!

CHOCTASTIC ICES

Extra equipment:
- electric whisk
- ice lolly moulds

Ingredients:
- 500 ml (17 fl.oz) double cream
- 1 vanilla pod, split
- 100 g (4 oz) caster sugar
- 150 ml (5 fl.oz) water
- 4 egg yolks
- 100 g (4 oz) milk or dark chocolate

1 Follow the instructions for the vanilla ice cream recipe on page 46 up to step 4. Continue to whisk the mixture until it thickens and is mousse-like.

2 Next, whisk in the cream and pour into a plastic tub. Place the tub into a freezer for an hour, then stir – the mixture should be partially frozen.

3 Then, pour the partially frozen ice cream into the lolly moulds. Put the moulds back in the freezer and let them set for a couple of hours, until solid.

4 Meanwhile, ask an adult to put a heatproof bowl over a saucepan of just-simmering water, making sure the bowl doesn't touch the water.

5 Break the chocolate into small pieces and put them into the bowl. Stir the mixture until the chocolate has melted. Pour the melted chocolate into a jug or large bowl and leave to cool.

6 Next, remove the ices from the freezer and let them stand at room temperature for 5 minutes. Then, remove from the moulds and dip the ices into the cooled chocolate, making sure they are completely covered.

7 Place the ices back into the freezer and leave to set for a couple of hours

8 Remove the ices from the freezer and let them stand at room temperature for 5 minutes. Then, remove from the moulds and enjoy!

TOP TIP!
Add chopped nuts to the melted chocolate for a great alternative!

SPRINKLE TOP POPS

TOP TIP!
Experiment with toppings! Why not try chopped nuts, marshmallows, honey or jam! Yum!

Extra equipment:
- ice lolly moulds
- blender
- sieve

Ingredients:
- 350 ml (12 fl.oz) milk
- 100 g (4 oz) caster sugar
- 1 teaspoon vanilla extract
- 255 g (9 oz) strawberries, washed and hulled
- 1 1/2 tablespoons clear honey
- 60 g (2 oz) milk chocolate
- sugar sprinkles

1 Ask an adult to place the milk and sugar in a pan and heat until the sugar dissolves. Next, stir in the vanilla extract and leave to cool.

2 Once cool, pour into the lolly moulds, leaving about a third at the top. Place into a freezer and let the lollies set for at least 4 hours, until solid.

3 Meanwhile, ask an adult to purée the strawberries in a blender. (If you have not got a blender, place the ingredients into a bowl and ask an adult to blend the mixture with a hand-held whisk.)

4 Then, carefully push the purée through a sieve and into a bowl.

5 Stir the honey into the purée. Then, pour the purée into each of the lolly moulds on top of the milk layer. Again, leave to set for at least 4 hours, until solid.

6 Ask an adult to put a heatproof bowl over a saucepan of just-simmering water, making sure the bowl doesn't touch the water. Break the chocolate into small pieces and put them into the bowl. Stir the mixture until the chocolate has melted. Let the chocolate cool for 8–10 minutes.

7 Remove a pop from its mould and dip the top of the pop into the chocolate, allowing any excess to drip onto a plate. Then, cover with sugar sprinkles. Repeat for each pop, and enjoy!

TRAFFIC LIGHT LOLLIES

Extra equipment:
- blender
- sieve
- ice lolly moulds

Ingredients:
- 350 ml (12 fl.oz) orange juice
- 3 large, ripe peaches or nectarines, peeled, stoned and sliced
- 4 ½ tablespoons runny honey
- 5 large kiwi fruit, peeled and sliced
- 100 ml (3 fl.oz) lemon juice
- 300 g (10 oz) caster sugar
- 1 lemon
- 255 g (9 oz) strawberries

1 First, pour a little of the orange juice into the bottom of the moulds, filling them to about a fifth. Place in a freezer and leave to set for about 4 hours.

2 Next, ask an adult to purée the nectarines or peaches in a blender. (If you have not got a blender, place the ingredients into a bowl and ask an adult to blend the mixture with a hand-held whisk.) Then, carefully push the purée through a sieve and into a bowl. Stir 1½ tablespoons of the honey into the purée. Then, pour the purée into each of the lolly moulds on top of the orange juice layer, again filling them to about a fifth. Place in a freezer to set.

3 Repeat the purée process for the kiwi layer, and add to the moulds.

4 Next, ask an adult to pour the sugar into a pan with 600 ml (20 fl.oz) of water. Heat gently until the sugar dissolves, then simmer for a couple of minutes. Stir in the lemon juice and then grate one lemon. Add the zest to the mixture, then leave to cool. Pour the mixture into the moulds, on top of the other layers, again filling them to about a fifth. Place in a freezer to set.

5 For the last layer, ask an adult to purée the strawberries in a blender, then add the remaining honey. Complete the lollies by adding the last layer, then freeze for at least 4 hours, until solid.

6 Remove the lollies from the freezer 5 minutes before eating. Enjoy!

TOP TIP!
If you would like the colours to be really bright, add a couple of drops of food colouring to each layer.

VANILLA ICE CREAM

Extra equipment:
- electric whisk
- ice cream maker (optional)

Ingredients:
- 500 ml (17 fl.oz) double cream
- 1 vanilla pod, split
- 100 g (4 oz) caster sugar
- 150 ml (5 fl.oz) water
- 4 egg yolks
- strawberries, to decorate
- mint leaves, to decorate

1 Ask an adult to heat the cream in a saucepan so that it almost boils and then remove from the heat. Add the split vanilla pod and leave it until the cream is completely cool.

2 Scrape the tiny seeds from the vanilla pod into the cream and remove the pod casing.

3 Dissolve the sugar in the water over a low heat. Then, ask an adult to turn up the heat and boil the mixture to create a light syrup. Leave the syrup mixture to cool for 1 minute.

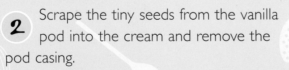

4 Place the egg yolks in a bowl and ask an adult to whisk them using an electric whisk, slowly adding the hot syrup.

5 Continue to whisk until the mixture thickens and is mousse-like. Then, whisk in the cream and pour into an ice cream maker and churn until frozen. Alternatively, if you don't have an ice cream maker you can freeze your ice cream in a plastic tub in the freezer. You will need to stir the mixture every hour to break up any ice.

6 Serve your ice cream when it's frozen.

TOP TIP! Serve your vanilla ice cream with strawberries and a mint leaf garnish.

STRAWBERRY ICE CREAM

Extra equipment:

- blender
- sieve
- ice cream maker (optional)

Ingredients:

- 350 g (12 oz) strawberries, hulled and roughly chopped
- 100 g (4 oz) caster sugar
- 2 egg yolks
- 300 ml (10 fl.oz) double cream
- wafer stick, to decorate

1 Ask an adult to purée the strawberries in a blender (reserving a couple for decoration), then sieve to remove any bits.

2 Put the caster sugar and egg yolks together in a bowl and whisk until thick.

3 Bring the cream to the boil in a saucepan and then gradually whisk it into the egg yolk mixture.

4 Pour the cream / egg yolk mixture back into the pan and cook over a low heat for 5 minutes, or until the mixture sticks to the back of a wooden spoon.

5 Strain the mixture into a bowl and add the strawberry purée.

6 Pour the mixture into an ice cream maker and churn until frozen. Alternatively, if you don't have an ice cream maker you can freeze your ice cream in a plastic tub in the freezer. You will need to stir the mixture every hour to break up any ice.

7 Serve your ice cream when it's frozen.

TOP TIP!
Serve with fresh strawberries and a wafer stick to give your ice cream the 'wow' factor!

47

CHOCOLATE ICE CREAM

TOP TIP! Why not serve the ice cream in a cone!

Extra equipment:
- electric whisk
- ice cream maker (optional)

Ingredients:
- 300 g (10 oz) dark chocolate, finely chopped
- 240 ml (8 fl.oz) milk
- 240 ml (8 fl.oz) double cream
- 175 g (6 oz) caster sugar
- 4 large egg yolks
- 150 ml (5 fl.oz) water

1 First, tip 200 g (7 oz) of dark chocolate into a heatproof bowl, reserving the rest to add to the ice cream later. Heat the milk, double cream and 25 g (1 oz) of caster sugar in a saucepan, then pour over the chocolate and stir until dissolved. Leave on one side until cool.

2 Ask an adult to whisk the egg yolks with an electric whisk and add this to the cooled chocolate cream mixture.

3 Next, place 150 g (5 oz) of sugar in a saucepan and add 150 ml (5 fl.oz) of water. Dissolve the sugar over a medium heat, stirring occasionally. Then, bring to a boil and cook for 5 minutes.

4 Ask an adult to pour the hot sugar syrup into the chocolate cream mixture, in a thin steady stream, whilst you whisk. Continue whisking until the mixture has thickened and is similar to a mousse – this should take about 5 minutes.

5 Add the extra chocolate and stir to blend everything together. Pour into an ice cream maker and churn until frozen. Alternatively, you could freeze the mixture in a tub, stirring it every hour to break up any ice and ensure that the chocolate is evenly mixed in.

6 Once it is frozen, scoop and serve!

CARAMEL ICE CREAM

Extra equipment:
- electric whisk
- ice cream maker (optional)

Ingredients:
- 100 g (4 oz) caster sugar
- 150 ml (5 fl.oz) water
- 2 egg yolks
- 300 ml (10 fl.oz) double cream
- chocolate strands, to decorate

1 Place the sugar and a third of the water in a saucepan. Stir over a medium heat until the sugar has dissolved.

2 Ask an adult to raise the heat and boil rapidly until a caramel syrup forms, then add the remaining water.

3 Whisk the yolks until they are a thick consistency. Then, slowly pour into the hot caramel, whisking continuously until the mixture is thick and cold.

4 Whisk the cream, until it is just beginning to thicken, and then carefully fold into the eggs and caramel.

5 Pour the mixture into an ice cream maker and churn until frozen. Alternatively, if you don't have an ice cream maker you can freeze your ice cream in a plastic tub in the freezer. You will need to stir the mixture every hour to break up any ice.

6 Serve when frozen.

TOP TIP!
Serve your ice cream with a sprinkle of yummy chocolate strands.

MINT CHOC-CHIP ICE CREAM

Extra equipment:
- plastic tub
- ice cream maker (optional)

Ingredients:
- 500 ml (17 fl.oz) milk
- 500 ml (17 fl.oz) double cream
- 200 g (7 oz) caster sugar
- 1 teaspoon vanilla extract
- 1 teaspoon peppermint extract
- 3 drops green food colouring (optional)
- 200 g (7 oz) milk chocolate, grated

1 In a large bowl, add the milk, cream, sugar, vanilla extract and peppermint extract. Stir well until the sugar has dissolved.

2 Next, add a few drops of the green food colouring (if you want your ice cream to look really green).

3 Pour into an ice cream maker and churn until partially frozen. Then, stir in the grated chocolate. Alternatively, if you don't have an ice cream maker you can freeze your ice cream in a plastic tub in the freezer. After an hour, mix in the chocolate, and then stir the mixture every hour to break up any ice.

4 Serve when frozen.

TOP TIP!
Ask an adult to dip the ice cream scoop into hot water – this will make it easier to serve!

HOT FUDGE ICE CREAM SUNDAE

Ingredients:

- 100 g (4 oz) butter
- 100 g (4 oz) demerara sugar
- 280 ml (10 fl.oz) double cream
- 4 scoops vanilla ice cream (see home-made recipe on p.46 or use shop-bought)
- 75 ml (3 fl.oz) whipped cream, to decorate
- pecans, to decorate (optional)

1 Ask an adult to melt the butter and demerara sugar in a pan. Simmer gently until the sugar has melted and the sauce begins to thicken and becomes dark brown and caramelised.

2 Remove from the heat and add the double cream carefully.

3 Reboil and simmer gently until the sauce is smooth and honey coloured. Remove from the heat and allow to cool (at this point the sauce will be very hot and dangerous to touch).

4 Pour a small amount of the sauce into the bottom of the sundae glass followed by a scoop of ice cream. Repeat the process again.

5 Top with whipped cream. Finish the sundae with a drizzle of the sauce and a sprinkle of pecans.

TOP TIP!
Why not double the ingredients to make extra helpings!

51

PECAN ICE CREAM SUNDAE

Extra equipment:
• baking tray

Ingredients:
• 4 scoops vanilla ice cream
  (see home-made recipe on
  p.46 or use shop-bought)
• pecans, to decorate

For the pecan brittle:
• 25 g (1 oz) pecans
• 3 tablespoons clear honey

For the hot chocolate sauce:
• 75 ml (3 fl.oz) double cream
• 25 g (1 oz) dark chocolate,
  roughly chopped

1 First, make the pecan brittle. Ask an adult to place the pecans in a frying pan with the honey and cook for 3–4 minutes until the honey starts to darken at the sides and the nuts are glazed.

2 Tip the pecans onto an oiled baking tray, cool, and roughly chop.

3 Next, make the hot chocolate sauce by melting the cream and chocolate together in a bowl over a pan of simmering water, making sure the bowl doesn't touch the water.

4 Pour a small amount of the hot chocolate sauce into a sundae glass and top with a sprinkling of pecan brittle, then a scoop of ice cream.

5 Repeat the layering process to finish, then top with a couple of whole pecans.

WARNING!
Contains nuts.

52

CHOCOLATE ICE CREAM SUNDAE

Extra equipment:
- whisk
- grater
- 2 sundae glasses
- piping bag

Ingredients:
- 4 scoops chocolate ice cream (see home-made recipe on p.48 or use shop-bought)
- 50 g (2 oz) milk chocolate, grated
- 75 ml (3 fl.oz) whipped cream, to decorate
- glacé cherries, to decorate

For the hot chocolate sauce:
- 15 g ($^1/_2$ oz) cornflour
- 280 ml (10 fl.oz) milk
- 15 g ($^1/_2$ oz) butter
- 50 g (2 oz) sugar
- 50 g (2 oz) dark chocolate

1 First, make the hot chocolate sauce. Mix the cornflour with a little milk.

2 Boil the remaining milk, whisk in the cornflour mixture and add the butter and sugar.

3 Reboil carefully and grate the dark chocolate into the hot (but not boiling) sauce, and whisk until smooth.

4 Pour a small amount of the hot chocolate sauce into each sundae glass and top with a sprinkling of grated milk chocolate, then a scoop of chocolate ice cream. Repeat the process until the glass is full.

5 Place the whipped cream into a piping bag and pipe it onto the top of the sundae.

6 Finish with a glacé cherry.

TOP TIP! Chopped nuts are a great addition to the cream topping.

BROWNIE ICE CREAM SUNDAE

Extra equipment:
- 20 cm (8 in) square cake tin
- greaseproof paper
- whisk

Ingredients:
- 2 eggs
- 240 g (8 oz) caster sugar
- 100 g (4 oz) butter
- 3 tablespoons cocoa powder
- 100 g (4 oz) self-raising flour
- 2 scoops vanilla ice cream

For the hot chocolate sauce:
- 15 g (½ oz) cornflour
- 280 ml (10 fl.oz) milk
- 15 g (½ oz) butter
- 50 g (2 oz) sugar
- 50 g (2 oz) dark chocolate
- sugar sprinkles, to decorate

1 Preheat the oven to 180°C / 350°F / gas mark 4.

2 To make the brownies, first, beat the eggs and the sugar together in a bowl. Ask an adult to melt the butter and beat in the cocoa powder before adding to the eggs and sugar.

3 Sift and then fold in the flour. Pour the mixture into a lined, greased cake tin. Bake for 40–45 minutes or until firm.

4 Once the topping is firm, cut the brownies into squares.

5 Now make the sauce. Mix the cornflour with a little milk.

6 Boil the remaining milk, whisk in the cornflour mixture and add the butter and sugar.

7 Reboil carefully and grate the dark chocolate into the hot (but not boiling) sauce, and whisk until smooth.

8 Place a brownie square on a plate. Place one scoop of vanilla ice cream on top and drizzle with the sauce. Top with sugar sprinkles to finish.

TOP TIP!
The brownies in this recipe also taste great by themselves!

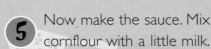

54

VANILLA MOUSSE WITH RASPBERRIES

Extra equipment:
- blender
- sieve
- individual cake rings

Ingredients:

For the mousse:
- 300 ml (10 fl.oz) whipping cream
- 15 g (½ oz) gelatine (leaf if possible)
- 150 g (5 ½ oz) fresh eggs (pasteurised if possible)
- 120 g (4 oz) caster sugar
- a few drops of vanilla essence

For the sauce:
- 360 g (13 oz) fresh raspberries
- 60 g (2 oz) icing sugar
- mint leaves, to decorate

1 To make the mousse, first beat the whipping cream until just before piping consistency.

2 Soak the gelatine in cold water, lift out the wet leaves and melt over a gentle heat.

3 Beat the eggs, sugar and vanilla until they are white and stiff, and beat in the melted gelatine.

4 Quickly fold in the whipped cream and spoon into individual greased cake rings. Level the tops and leave to set in the fridge.

5 Select the best raspberries for decoration (about 6–8 for each mousse).

6 For the sauce, ask an adult to liquidise the remaining fruit and blend in most of the icing sugar. When smooth and shiny, strain to remove the pips.

7 Place each mousse on a plate, run a small knife blade around the mould and lift off carefully.

8 Arrange the raspberries on the top of each mousse and pour the raspberry sauce around the outside.

9 Decorate with a mint leaf to finish.

TOP TIP! This vanilla mousse also works well with strawberries!

LEMON & RASPBERRY BOMBE

TOP TIP!
To serve, dip the bowl into luke warm water for a few seconds, to loosen the bombe.

SERVES 6-8

Extra equipment:
- whisk
- sieve
- freezer-proof bowl
- 1.25 litre (40 fl.oz) bombe mould or pudding basin

Ingredients:
- 2 eggs (separated)
- 250 g (9 oz) caster sugar
- 300 ml (10 fl.oz) double cream
- finely grated zest of 2 lemons
- juice of 3 lemons
- 170 g (6 oz) raspberries
- grated rind and juice of 1 orange
- a few fresh raspberries, to decorate
- whipped cream, to decorate
- sprig of mint, to decorate

1 Ask an adult to whisk half the egg whites until stiff. Then, whisk in half of the sugar and the egg yolks.

2 In a separate bowl, beat half of the cream until thick, and add the lemon zest and juice. Next, fold into the egg mixture and pour into a freezer-proof bowl. Freeze until firm.

3 Place the raspberries in a saucepan with the remaining sugar, orange rind and juice, and poach for 4–5 minutes.

4 Set aside half of the raspberries. Then, strain the remaining fruit through a sieve and chill. Ask an adult to whip the remaining cream and fold into the purée, followed by the raspberries.

5 Whisk the remaining egg whites until stiff and fold into the mixture. Freeze until firm.

6 Chill a 1.25 litre (40 fl.oz) bombe mould or pudding basin. Remove the lemon ice cream from the freezer-proof bowl and line the bombe mould with it. Cover and freeze for one hour. Fill the centre with the raspberry mixture and freeze until firm.

7 Unmould onto a plate. Cut into wedges and decorate with raspberries, whipped cream and mint leaves.

MIXED BERRY SORBET

Extra equipment:
- blender
- sieve
- ice cream maker (optional)

Ingredients:
- 100 g (4 oz) caster sugar
- 180 ml (6 fl.oz) water
- 2 teaspoons glucose syrup
- 450 g (1 lb) mixed berries, (fresh or frozen), reserving some for decoration
- squeeze of lemon juice
- sugar sprinkles, to decorate

1 Pour the sugar, 100 ml (3 fl.oz) of the water and the glucose syrup into a saucepan. Ask an adult to dissolve the sugar over a medium heat without stirring. Bring to the boil and simmer briskly for 5–7 minutes until the mixture thickens to a syrup. Remove from the heat, pour into a bowl and leave to cool.

2 Put the mixed berries in another saucepan. Squeeze some lemon juice over them and simmer over a low heat for a minute or two until soft.

3 Put the mixed berries in a blender and ask an adult to whizz until smooth. Then, push the purée through a fine sieve to remove all of the seeds.

4 Add the cooled syrup and remaining water to the purée and whisk together.

5 Pour the mixture into an ice cream maker and churn until frozen. Alternatively, if you don't have an ice cream maker you can freeze your sorbet in a plastic tub in a freezer.

6 Once frozen, scoop into a glass. Garnish with some leftover berries, some sugar sprinkles and a cool cocktail decoration.

TOP TIP! These are great for sleepovers or parties. Make them in advance, then freeze until needed!

57

ORANGE SORBET

Extra equipment:
- grater
- ice cream maker (optional)

Ingredients:
- 500 ml (½ pt) water
- 200 g (7 oz) caster sugar
- 4 large oranges
- 2 tablespoons orange juice

1 Ask an adult to heat the water and sugar in a saucepan, being careful not to boil the mixture. Stir for 2 minutes until the mixture is syrup-like in texture, then transfer to a bowl to cool.

2 Grate the rind from two of the oranges and squeeze the juice from four, reserving four halved orange skins for later. Mix the juice and rind in a bowl, then stir the extra orange juice into the cooled sugar syrup, followed by the juice and rind mixture.

3 Cover, then leave to chill in the fridge for an hour.

4 Next, pour the mixture into an ice cream maker and churn until frozen. Alternatively, if you don't have an ice cream maker you can freeze the sorbet in a plastic tub in a freezer.

5 Once frozen, scoop the sorbet into the reserved orange halves. Garnish with a few rind ribbons (ask an adult to grate these) to finish.

TOP TIP!
Presenting sorbets in their skins looks great! Try doing this with the lemon sorbet too!

STRAWBERRY SORBET

Extra equipment:
- blender
- sieve
- ice cream maker (optional)

Ingredients:
- 160 ml (5 1/2 oz) water
- 135 g (5 oz) granulated white sugar
- 1 kg (2 lbs) fresh or frozen strawberries
- 2 tablespoons lemon juice
- mint leaves, for decoration

1 Ask an adult to heat the water and sugar in a saucepan, being careful not to boil the mixture. Stir for 2 minutes until the mixture is syrup-like in texture, then transfer to a bowl to cool, then chill in the fridge.

2 Meanwhile, thaw the strawberries if using frozen, then ask an adult to place them in a blender, along with the lemon juice and process until smooth. Then, push the purée through a sieve to remove the pips.

3 Place the mixture in a bowl and chill in the fridge.

4 Once both mixtures have chilled, combine them together.

5 Next, pour the mixture into an ice cream maker and churn until frozen. Alternatively, if you don't have an ice cream maker you can freeze the sorbet in a plastic tub in a freezer.

6 Once frozen, scoop into a glass and garnish with a mint leaf.

TOP TIP!
Enjoy this refreshing sorbet after a large meal — it will cleanse your palette!

59

PEACHES AND CREAM ICE CREAM

SERVES 6-8

TOP TIP!
Decorate with extra peach chunks and a sprig of mint!

Extra equipment:

- blender
- ice cream maker (optional)

Ingredients:

- 568 ml (20 fl.oz) carton double cream
- 300 ml (½ pt) whole milk
- ½ vanilla pod, split
- 6 large egg yolks
- 50 g (2 oz) caster sugar
- 5 peaches, cut into chunks
- mint leaves, to decorate

1 Ask an adult to heat the double cream, milk and vanilla pod in a saucepan, being careful not to boil the mixture. Next, beat the egg yolks and sugar together in a bowl. Remove the vanilla pod from the cream mixture, then pour into the sugar and egg mixture, stirring constantly.

2 Transfer the mixture back into the saucepan and heat for 10–12 minutes, stirring gently until the mixture has a custard-like texture. Transfer to a bowl to cool, then chill in the fridge.

3 Next, pour the mixture into an ice cream maker and churn until it is extremely thick, but not fully frozen. Alternatively, if you don't have an ice cream maker you can freeze your ice cream in a plastic tub in the freezer. You will need to stir the mixture every hour to break up any ice, until the ice cream is extremely thick, but not fully frozen.

4 Meanwhile, ask an adult to pour the peach chunks, reserving some for decoration, into a blender and process until smooth.

5 Then, spoon the peach purée into the ice cream, using the spoon to make a ripple effect. Transfer the ice cream back to the freezer and leave it to set overnight.

6 Serve your ice cream when it's frozen.

ZINGY LIME ICE CREAM

Extra equipment:
• ice cream maker (optional)

Ingredients:
• 250 ml (8 fl.oz) milk
• 175 ml (6 fl.oz) whipping cream
• 200 g (7 oz) sugar
• zest of 2 or 3 limes
• 175 ml (6 fl.oz) fresh lime juice
• a few drops of green food colouring (optional)

1 Ask an adult to heat the milk, cream and sugar in a saucepan, being careful not to boil the mixture. Stir for 2 minutes until the sugar has dissolved, then transfer to a bowl.

2 Add the lime zest, juice and food colouring to the mixture, and stir. Leave the mixture to cool, then chill in the fridge.

3 Next, pour the mixture into an ice cream maker and churn until frozen. Alternatively, if you don't have an ice cream maker you can freeze your ice cream in a plastic tub in the freezer. You will need to stir the mixture every hour to break up any ice.

4 Once frozen, scoop into colourful glasses and add a couple of spoon straws!

TOP TIP! Make this ice cream extra zingy by making it lemon and lime – just add the juice and zest of one lemon!

RASPBERRY RIPPLE ICE CREAM

TOP TIP!
Decorate with extra raspberries and a sprig of mint!

SERVES 6-8

Extra equipment:
- ice cream maker (optional)
- blender
- sieve

Ingredients:
- 568 ml (20 fl.oz) carton double cream
- 300 ml (1/2 pt) whole milk
- 1/2 vanilla pod, split
- 6 large egg yolks
- 50 g (2 oz) caster sugar
- 300 g (10 1/2 oz) raspberries, plus extra for decoration
- icing sugar, to taste
- mint leaves, to decorate

1 Ask an adult to heat the double cream, milk and vanilla pod in a saucepan, being careful not to boil the mixture. Next, beat the egg yolks and sugar together in a bowl. Remove the vanilla pod from the cream mixture, then pour into the sugar and egg mixture, stirring constantly.

2 Transfer the mixture back into the saucepan and heat for 10–12 minutes, stirring gently until the mixture is custard-like. Transfer to a bowl to cool, then chill in the fridge.

3 Next, pour the mixture into an ice cream maker and churn until it is extremely thick, but not fully frozen. Alternatively, if you don't have an ice cream maker you can freeze your ice cream in a plastic tub in the freezer. You will need to stir the mixture every hour to break up any ice, until the ice cream is extremely thick, but not fully frozen.

4 Meanwhile, ask an adult to pour the raspberries, reserving some for decoration, into a blender and process until smooth. Then, push the raspberry purée through a sieve to remove any pips.

5 Then, spoon the raspberry purée into the ice cream, using the spoon to make a ripple effect. Transfer the ice cream back to the freezer and leave it to set overnight.

6 Serve your raspberry ripple ice cream when it's frozen.

PINEAPPLE ICE CREAM

Extra equipment:
- blender
- ice cream maker (optional)

Ingredients:
- 1 lemon
- 450 g (1 lb) fresh pineapple, cut into chunks
- 450 ml (16 fl.oz) water
- 175 g (6 oz) sugar
- 300 ml (1/2 pt) double cream

1 First, ask an adult to grate the rind from the lemon, then squeeze it, reserving the juice for later.

2 Then, ask an adult to place the pineapple in a blender and process until smooth. Transfer to a bowl.

3 Next, ask an adult to heat the water and sugar in a saucepan, being careful not to boil the mixture. Stir for 2 minutes until the mixture is syrup-like in texture, then add the lemon rind. Transfer to a bowl to cool, then chill in the fridge.

4 Combine the puréed pineapple and lemon juice together and mix with an equal amount of the cooled sugar syrup.

5 Whisk the double cream and then carefully fold it into the fruit purée.

6 Then, pour the mixture into an ice cream maker and churn until frozen. Alternatively, if you don't have an ice cream maker you can freeze your ice cream in a plastic tub in the freezer. You will need to stir the mixture every hour to break up any ice.

7 Serve your pineapple ice cream when it's frozen.

TOP TIP! Drizzle with chocolate sauce and scoop into an ice cream cone!

INDEX OF RECIPES

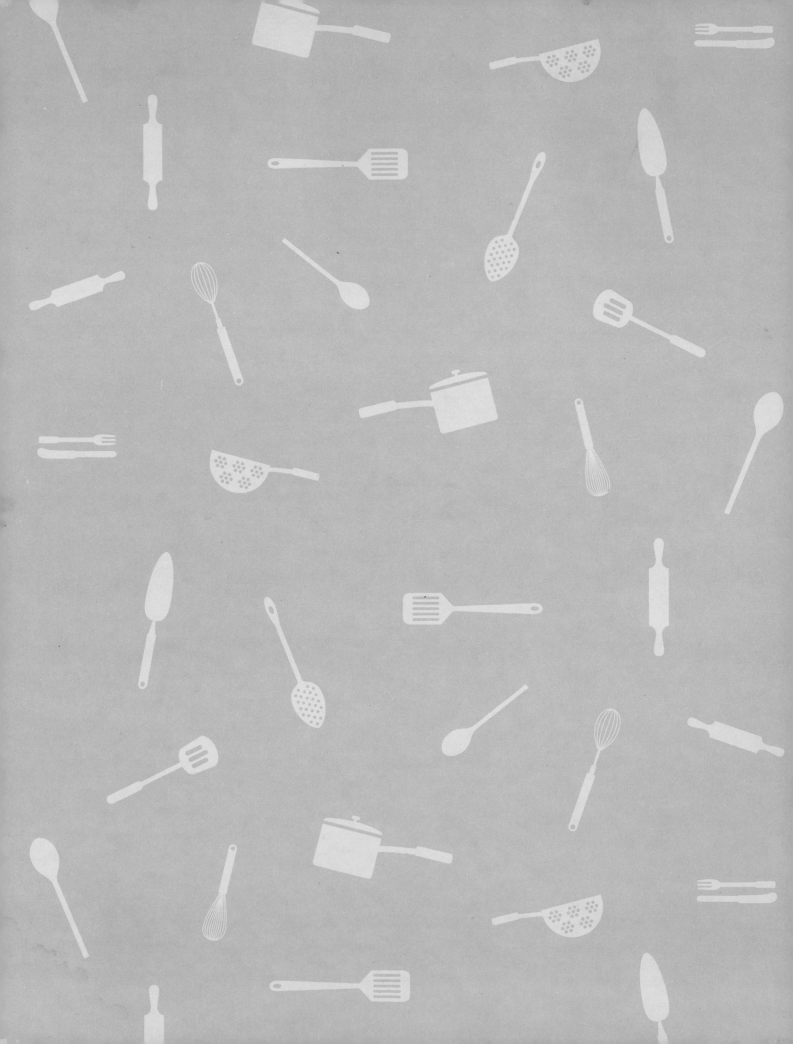